on the ground

T0048835

on the ground

FANNY HOWE

GRAYWOLF PRESS
Saint Paul, Minnesota

Publication of this volume is made possible in part by a grant provided by
the Minnesota State Arts Board, through an appropriation by the Minnesota
State Legislature; a grant from the Wells Fargo Foundation Minnesota; and
a grant from the National Endowment for the Arts, which believes that a
great nation deserves great art. Significant support has also been provided by
the Bush Foundation; Target, Marshall Field's and Mervyn's with support
from the Target Foundation; the McKnight Foundation; and other generous
contributions from foundations, corporations, and individuals. To these
organizations and individuals we offer our heartfelt thanks.

MINNESOTA
STATE ARTS BOARD

NATIONAL
ENDOWMENT
FOR THE ARTS

Published by Graywolf Press
2402 University Avenue, Suite 203
Saint Paul, Minnesota 55114
All rights reserved.

www.graywolfpress.org

Published in the United States of America

ISBN 1-55597-403-1

2 4 6 8 9 7 5 3 1
First Graywolf Printing, 2004

Library of Congress Control Number: 2003112164

Many thanks to those editors who published some of these poems in *Can We
Have Our Ball Back?*, the *Columbia Review, Colorado Review, Poetry Ireland,
Grand Street, Post-Apollo Press* ("Forged"), *Lyric,* the *Poker,* and *Golden
Handcuffs.*

Cover design: Kyle G. Hunter

Cover art: Helen Chadwick, *Viral Landscape No. 3* (detail)
　　　　　Copyright Helen Chadwick Estate

contents

on the ground

Far and Near

Small silver face out of the gray

I call it a deer in a phantom forest
Baader-Meinhof with a future

Smoke of assassination
Burning of oil

Maybe it's trees that have broken away
Or clouds around them

A dragon-shaped smear on a window

But there is a moment of clarity
When nothing is out there

Now I call it an asshole
In fiery red clothing

Light shoots from its finger
Like wind with hair

Is it an alien cowering
In the rape robe of war?

Mother and child on an icy globe?

Or just the eyes of day

The World Bank

How did you get here?

The shuttle from London

I'm not getting involved
but what father sent you?

What father? What London

You should've missed your plane
Are you afraid on the eve of night?

Dear Lord! I had wanted to see truth
while I was alive
so why did you send me these tickets instead?
Seagulls can't even fly this high

If it rains, my hands will be wet

With unreal gentleness
Generals

mounted the hill
"Mind, now. Mud."

One sighed like a serpent on an empty egg
but it was really military thinking:

travel casket round trip

He brought his ashes home

His whose? His own?

His ashes: *his* hair and chest
And bones
Does it matter whose?

He brought his home

She brought *hers*

These words alone could distinguish them

Not to say his way
was not her way
but she said existential is my religion
and in fear looked at herself

"who am now" "who has outlived"

both him and then.

No agonizing thread through sex in dark beds

can block out the cars and tanks

Milligrams of pills for different fears instead

Flocks of birds and cherubim
almost get chopped by a helicopter

and gladness is yours when they survive

Don't abandon your soul the child
who breathes
inside your skin, three in one

points of vision
meet geometry on this sheet

Chosen and did choose
to fly that way that day

Should I have to tell you what I mean?
You can't err symbolically

With a thud and a scrape
on a snow carpet
worn to something hard

shhh the wind was mothering

But who's the mother here anyway?
The rock, the moan, Mary or the air?

No and was ashamed
she had refused him

To have been a Wife—awful—
but not this worse nothing

like lamb with smoky burning
it was her Easter Requiem

Mentally washed his body: cold toes and fingering inlets
groin and back of ears up the numb legs, soft chest down
scrubbed crotch and anus
gums and bare tongue (white) soaped the testicles
and squeezed his member for some little firelight

Anything mechanical from a ghost?

From here the sky over Former Yugoslavia
looks both formal and forlorn
like clergy trying to turn rocks into the host

Croatia, Holy Week: 1996. On a 45-minute flight to Dubrovnik
from Tuzla—on the Dalmation Coast—Americans for the World
Bank crashed. Heavy rains, gusting winds, the Adriatic Sea gray
near Plat.

The past is unrecognized rubble
At least that's how it came to meet him

The pop of a lightbulb in the bulkhead

Now a big black bonnet
has landed in a tree and all us co-hearts
are left chilling

D—th = perfect math

elective affinity
where body and mind are combustible

in the choice work-furnace

Satan says things that don't make sense
like "The planes were delayed and so they crashed."

Now muddy starlings flock around
the salt-sad lagoons

A green canoe or dirty lock
conjure up someone

posted as lost or ghost
as far away as: "Have you seen him on Canal Street?"

An angel is a messenger who runs very fast
so you don't see angels anymore

Time has altered its arc
And angels keep changing form and never pause

Their wings might be as sharp as missiles
That can mimic

The vicious acts of human beings. Look at the clouds

The mist is dispersing
and Baby Blue is faceless without words

Fold over white
around my winter bed

Setting is always telling me
you can't keep a thing

Not even the night freeze
across the sheets

Even that accommodates

The men in a barge took his clothes away

The children cried, they understood
"You won't see love again."

The lagoon to the cut was thick and brown
and someone sang

"Your heart was split
You didn't know
Who you loved, or if."

The barge drifted south with artillery on it

Our bodies were an offering—anyone could tell—
to the bulging sky
while our sheets were like skins of suffering

Woe to those women
broken at twenty
useful at forty

Woe to us
when we combine
production with recollection

The pile on the skyline
is gun-metal bright

(not olive trees alive and silver)

if the men who describe them are right

He was laid on a flag-draped catafalque
in America—just one among many

sacrificed to the worst atrocity
in Europe since the forties

Young African American, broken
on the back of St. John's Hill

for the sake of economics

Like sparrows having striven

unavailing in their chests

even corporations with living wills
don't survive
zero visibility

No credit

Executive into infinity

Forged

I always knew I had no right to be
Eating filling becoming wept

Sold by tickets to this trip myself
A fiction as fixed as the crucifixion
or tracks hammered into banked quarters

where logic can carry you to hell
but gives a spatial unity that in essence is emotional

Did I have faith or was it hype

Q of changing names and physical fates
Erasure calling from the lips
No sleep! An end constructed as an opening

When a self has no rights
in relation to its words but bears false witness
from a block of slush and Christmas drinks

Why every day such levity

Successive déjà vus
ended then remembered
overlapping since leaving
the building materials of sequential plot

Behind time thickens and deepens
while eyes grow blind in cosmic winds

Made tracks to King's Cross
Bricks stretched to breaking
as bird wings in the brambles do

Transport via red-doored stations
past candle-tipped Muslim lettering
to jewels from the East End
where everything stiff is shining

At Westminster missed Mass
—"More memory of Paul; of nature less"—

someone gave a warehouse-wide yell
over flyers on saints and pilgrimage

bought a hat got a life
since everything looks like it's waiting to end
except for the stuff that's not made by hand

Pitch in a poet in the alley a board
A leaning rod a thrown cloth
seems to signify a man huddled but faceless
A thick ruined guest with his paper cup
extended torn sneakers
reading Upanishads to each of us
Just 7 percent of our being visible

Once in a red hermitage and Indian's cabin

flies, dry-throated birds and black ashes
where there used to be grass

No water but the shafts of pastels
On dry banks a sky blue insect
lounged its being blind
to all the simple rules of blindness

To prison camps like low cow barracks
On wheels the rusty tracks and worn treads
Tufted lumps of earth stuffed with grass

Those garlands we passed whose yards really
were traces of working wills

Rolling hills slashed by dull buildings
severed this path to the mystic heart of red

Yes luck we cause and pleasures too

What else do I know after the blessing
of labor's silence traffic blocked
locked shops—cafés open—orange inside

At parts of the center the sweets and news
are placed to help you suffer living
in mouth and eyes

Wet shoes drain the aches from human faces
as wood leaks ashes

On the dank wet streets the Parcel Force
drives slow and licensed betting
supports the way remorse can happen

And a person's not made of shit but dirt
as long as the name of God can just come first

Determined by day by need
Multiple bodies parceled into files
Computers chiming cheerfully without appetite

All of us seem to be transfixed
stacked as we are facing east
week after week a little like
one of the ones who were invited to life

Green leaves form shells
of white light not paper

Personality likewise imitates
fakery like this
Eclipse of the apocalypse head
on a circle likened to an "O they said
Earth is a good name for home."

London's seven prisons
for seven sins in seven days

Several unrecorded yelps
each spent like the flap
of a bird taking off claws shoved up

over Wandsworth Brixton Latchmere
Belmarsh Holloway Pentonville and Wormwood Scrubs

I should have been happier yesterday
but was dispatched by fate otherwise

An iron broom brushed away
a length of malaise and my fear
like a visitor
carrying something edible to a prisoner
counted each crumb as it disappeared

Part of the world's much earlier than this

It's where the crib is what they call the crèche

Traumatized by time
one moves with terrific will a wedding dress
is carrying heroically a continuum
given to one experience
that otherwise had no place to lay its head

That isn't love which lacks compassion
but fruit splattered on a platform

It must be the case that the train
is this century's model Cross

On the left side a sea of fields sticks furrows
stations and moving baby sheep

On the right eyeless twilight doesn't blink

Preserve her loneliness in a long red jar
away from London's film-tinted sky

Walk along mud meadow spindleberries
white snowballs on twigs and the winter cherry
still winging flowers
near five red roses solid with cold

Alien fish like souls must sleep in such a chill

Rosejuice from a novice bouquet
Poetry pure liquid at the core
of something sweet and short

Is a rose already pink inside its idiot dirt

Does a full heart carry the whole girl
when the will has been transformed to love
and certain acts absorbed

Her guest is coming as a child
from gray railroad clouds
through weak sprays of cherryflowers

whose transport in a closed position
is an entrance folding over
into mobile images
copying plates on evolution

Did I believe or was it hope
Like a fir tree in a children's nursery
candlelights on thistleballs
at a village called Manningtree

Funny how children continue to call Mummy
to a woman and her law at a table
that she may turn all words back into the prayers
                that they once were

Grind and forge
for minimal spark and speed

Time is so intimate

Then it is finished
and on you go burning to a cinder
A forgery in figure only
Signature cut to the wheels.

(for Annlucien)

9/11

The first person is an existentialist

like trash in the groin of the sand dunes
like a brown cardboard home beside a dam

like seeing like things the same
between Death Valley and the desert of Paran

An earthquake a turret with arms and legs
The second person is the beloved

like winners taking the hit
like looking down on Utah as if

it was Saudi Arabia or Pakistan
like war-planes out of Miramar

like a split cult a jolt of coke New York
like Mexico in its deep beige couplets

like this, like that . . . like Call us all It
Thou It. "Sky to Spirit! Call us all It!"

The third person is a materialist.

2002

We are stamping on the bosom of Satan, boot-boot

We are sure of the origins of evil

Ice-chop. Man and soil
Which came first? The robin or the worm?

Burst a well, *das kapital,* sell, sell

The windows into the worm are flowers

Lily layers and a basket upright

Its stick figure is like a piece

Of something that can't stop living

Severed from nothing at both ends

Wish on the first worm of the year
and all other firsts as ways to get
what you want. The first fish-hook, the first bait

The first time you hear a woodchuck being its name

When the president wakes up, it always asks
What am I doing here? Where's that man?

Satan broke open the worm
One night on the Dalmatian coast
And out of the grass came another worm
and another, or was it a word by then

Hatch, hatch, snake of snake

Plague came and went in a matter of days
Town to town and the saved
got out of there fast

Tongues of grass curled around their legs

For the others, suck suck on the man's breast

How utopian is water
when you are disordered or bloody from a fall
Everyone loves the way Satan
mixes water with his syntax

A plug of magnolia budding too soon

A long blue sky without a brow

No providence
but a grope in the galley of simultaneity

Poor us. Here but not why
It's the proximity problem, being stuck
inside a body unknown to it or anyone

So the sticking to things, associations
No way to free dog
or color from surrounding whys

This about existence, paper-littered river
and the first wish. Wish, wish, water

The Long Wrong

When the cold-blooded are proved right
—judgment secure—case complete
we will first see a tangle
of close-ups—gourd and gold

and apples still rotten
rugosa roses down to three petals only
and each holocaust will be an ant heap

All the little wrongs will come into focus

But who will be glad about this?

Even the bigamists
who thought they were splitting
each lie into fragments
too small to be located

might find their trail is following them

And the shortsighted whose faces
are a blur of glee
may begin to establish shapes
around pockets of light and air
in the thicket they are part of

but they won't sense the force
that gathers those shapes
into actual consequence
until they themselves can't go forward

And neither will the hesitant
experience their weakness
as an ability—I don't think—
until it gathers into a body
of uncertainties that has influence

When the one big cruelty comes down on us
out of a seeming emptiness

it will be a helium packed with the force
of freely given evasions

so if some still believe
that the cold-blooded alone are responsible
for this power
how will they show that it came from elsewhere

Nothing has increased

The Dragon of History

I have seen it happen
A face with fangs and gills

represents history and an angel
is beating the beast on the back

Both are made of marble
One is a dragon

Its head is flat
like the iron tanks
in muddy water
that drove the men into the Gulf of Tonkin.

The dragon of history
generates its own assistants
who take a chain of hairs
wired to a clip and pull up

dreamy stuff
and analyze it
toward a theory of uselessness

All of them groaning
"The cost of it!"

No tide that cries *Have life!*
is left in a drain
where fish have soft gums

They have been overcome
by Marketplace

Slime floats like a hubcap
in a stink of gas and rusty hooks

The original dragon contains in its skin
a curve of generations
and their achievements

They disperse like particles
of something never whole

A museum of grass and logs
watched over and gobbled up

to produce more appetite and fuel

Physical history
is the repository of memory, its cubes of DNA
fuel it
and are it

History patterns the brain like Byzantine tiles
while science studies the sky
and art looks to the sides

You can build a fortress
to protect an idea of kindness

(Dragons one way, camels the other)

but lose the war
because of the idea
though not the trace of its structure

The dragon is flesh at first
and lives on what it measures
devours and regurgitates

But sometimes someone escapes
with no memory
and can start fresh

In my experience

the angel with his wings up
is trying to kill the dragon of history

to prove that air
is stronger than the objects in it

and if he wasn't made of stone, he would.

On the Ground

Satan fell behind, it was a taxi's shadow
where Man put his foot on the sidewalk

His mouth covered mine and he was gone

Italo once said a kiss on the mouth is the sign of betrayal
and pointed at Judas in the painting

(his muscular hand, his brush)

There was an ache in the canvas he had speared himself

That was the day when rain fell until twelve
outside the studio and twelve months before that shadow

Not a rink but ashed-over ice
Rain on a windshield, a green light

Apartments made of dirt, neon
hangers outlined in the cleaner's window

I think proximity is the abyss
between God and us because

every fabric of my body is trying
to know why saying

I love you
in a time of extremity is a necessity

Dreams before waking are eyes into the future
where there is no Zurich but an alphabet

beginning with Z
so go away before I ask to know

what you mean about wanting to go

Terrified of being first?
of being dirt?

Of being ambushed or embossed? Personally
I want to batter my way out of this cage of psychology

and get to the longing I really know about

Morning dusk—his figure furry

Threads of gray hair

and outside, a world without a leader
Oil and land mines

Lonely words scurrying to work

If the dark bricks hide criminal life
so does each body

dedicated to maintaining power
by suppressing its delights

Inside this egg the walls are lacquered blue

Creamy tones of windowsill
and slat. Dawn from hell on up

I hear a rooster deny, deny, deny
or is it Man

Lies smell in every detail
as the light increases in this shell

Maybe the end of the world happened long ago
A whirl as quick as Judas breaking his neck
and every sound is an echo

Poor love in the order of existence

subsists on passivity inside this skin
where pain has cut a pattern

and a red heart's a little devil
speared by its own hand

and the brain of this stranger—
is it mine or its own—and its skeleton?

Can I toss them aside
like an armful of sticks and set out as a feeling
to find Hana and Issa across the night

Happiness has become unbearable
so don't stay with me

Ilona said this from the hall

Doors are here for both ways of walking

The split bed and bodies facing
where two unanimities
make a positive zero

She was hoping to die into Hans
so I left her house

I thought I was happy and said to my friend

It's because we are together

The blushing hills were rusty
its nerves as icy as his sleeves

Doll's hair, snow like artificial
Elimination of detail, a day to be grateful

He had broken parole

With speed-thinning strides
a horse passed by without a saddle

A body never forgets
The lens is turned on its own tremendum

Only blocks away—tubes, needles, straps
at the physician's prison

No sign of reflection, just blood and bone
trying to incorporate meds into atoms

When the body escapes without identification
this is its identification:

Chunks of moonstone smoothing a curb
Honey night snow in the city

She swept up my hair from the linoleum floor
and shook out the sheet

A rouge along the shades and drinks to be drunk

In transit, in transit, in stations and camps

little white spots wobbled from wall to phone

Star-lashes batted

—it was truck lights exiting the pike
and other war zones

Farther wars report on us:

an arsenal of artworks and theories
that contribute to the power of the military

"Beware of the fruits of your labor!"

My father was a soldier
who was smaller than my son

when he returned as a ghost.

I begged him to stay with us
but he said: "Not until you come to life."

Medjugorje

Mary held Jesus
Then calm came through

He was a man lying down
so there was a long-term reason why

she held still, but also

figs and catathetic cries
on his empty side

made her sigh: "In the small arms of a child
I was held and justified

It was better than temple
or life inside an urn
thin and streamlined for an institution.

I keep reproducing
the hallelujahs of the fruits of the womb

before they die."

I wish I was Jesus
with baby Mary
a gold string theory
built out of twos!

I wish I was that yellow
strand that dribbled
like spittle
into the people's eyes

because it was a person
without a name
and God roared down
This is the second and last time!

The theological lamb
grins at the Sunday rite

It sees the good
in something missing

—its birth unviolent

since Mary's eardrum
was her hymen

Cluck into the oven, Biddy,
while Jesus takes the baby

and lays her in a little crib

Its slats are made of honey
Its sheets are parchment

Orange as marmalade
in a crushed sugar shell

Brahman is a condiment
sweet but cold

Mary can play in her bed-cap
nibbling when necessary

Mary did a funny thing

She made an empty plane
for Yogananda
to play with in the park

His park
above water
—fruits of many colors
with no air in them

Electromagnetic
squinted at the sea
fuzzily

His throw was how the volume
of the empty form
gathered color and value

and also the way Yogananda
played India with this plane
in Yugoslavia

across the ruins

and never called *mine!*

gave it wings

(for Danzy)

Kneeling Bus

My church the bus
is padded with shadows

Wing-colors in winter
Sky like fractured smoke

So many corpses
to cope with
The white sheets
Infirmities bandaged

Wool-capped heads
and wheelchairs
in the back of the M11
February, 2003.

A billiards bar
where a forest was
a nocturnal factory

past the Petrossian
restaurant building
snow white stone work

A mitten is pressed
by a nanny at 67th and Columbus.

Twins of anything are frightening
They ask for it

Morning white night

A fistful of snow or crack cocaine
Two buses sigh into a single stop

One driver unzips the door
and lowers the lift outside

Artificial light is staring
at two eyes weeping inside the bus

You see, parts don't add up when love is missing.

The fire in our sorrows
warmed the sheets

That fire was worth a cord
of wood

Nothing was agreed upon
between us

but that ashy heat, raw nerve

No green card, no compensation,
no visa or free meal

Not even a postage stamp
and not the spit for it

No reassurance but tribal heat
and one agreement

to be buried together.

Satan announces himself without sense
I am pro-life, I kill from a distance.

Now muddy pigeons flock around
Battery Park

A green cab or sticky lock
conjures up someone

posted as lost or ghost
Have you seen his dog tag at least?

Never trust holiness on a face

God is calling for God
inside bodies and caves.

This has to happen at the exact same minute:

The people get better
The people improve
The people are hopeful
and they hate war
The people understand
that they are the law

The people are good
The people are tender
The people are just
and merciful to each other
The people are friends
and unafraid of each other

All this has to happen to everyone without exception.
Now answer these questions:

Why is the messiah dumped in a pit?
Why is the messiah scorned and laughed at?
Why does the messiah wear his heart
on his chest and then point at it?

No answer. That's why.

Hymn of the hidden
plays for itself alone

Hymn of the hidden
has colorful rhythms

Jupiter rolls by like a penny

My secret eye sees it

Here ride my desperate ones
I am desperate too

A pterodactyl
in a yellow sky

Immigration of feathers
to Armageddon

Self-annihilation

is required for salvation
in faraway Pondicherry.

So I'll be the clerk
I'll polish the apples

once you have said
that you really meant it:

"Citizen, I meant it."

I'll never write a villanelle
but a chorus of spirals

to muck up your wars

I'll defy emptiness
instead of dying

I'll follow Jesus onto the M11
with my sack of apples

and smile like the nanny
at 67th and Columbus

in fake fur and dark glasses,
a child's hand in hers.

Like the Sabbath when sheep and brute

are equal being without use

Like an etching of animals

on the same glass sheet: cows, goats,

a dog or two pretending to be far away

Like the seventy-two virgins

remaining as they are through eternity

and the attendant men beside them

Which came first, evil or the law?
Messianic time is the time of neither.

Then I saw one in the back

bearded, deranged, trashed

Depreciation
of self-interest

Long on loss, the band
of pain
around his mind

I could feel it.
He was in this sense angelic:

a map of Gaza
its pavement split
by degrees of violence

in a flat universe

Then I saw four of him
en route to Qatar
each leaning in
another direction
without one face

And for one unable to hear
noise was what they were
not saying to each other
being one thing
on a piece of glass.

Is the only way to survive
to run or compromise

Is it wishful homicide
when you a let a man walk up and shoot
the woman beside you?

Her soft-brown hand in yours,
a shawl around her face.

Blood painted a line on the floor
to where the ambush began.

She knew they were coming
but had something to tell them.

So this is what we were traveling for!

They called her Granny with one voice.

Murder or suicide
depending on which side we collapsed.

Rock buildings wobbled into rubble
and then got up again.

Where is everyone

when I am alone
with the driver

Is my recent loss
the cause of those footsteps

clicking to the sidewalk

Once the air was thick with links
that darted and jerked

refracting whatever
flashings of eye

were captured in its light

Now I think the dance of separated things
never began never being

Oh God, especially tonight!

"Och brother your sister died
Och how your sister cried
Och horrors your sister took a knife
Och how your sister writhed
and prayed in a stranger's room.

Turn back time!
Let's start that day again.

The baby is bundled in warm cotton,
he is sitting upright and smiling
You can't tell
when the baby will smile
but you can tell
when he's warm and fed. Dear baby
little boy, little fate, sweet baby yours is the world.

Love is triumphant
when Love is welcomed. If love doesn't come
when love is calling, if Love
doesn't answer the call to itself,
the soul revolts and grows cold,
the mind goes around and around and can't get out.
Love owns the body and the mind but Och no!

It can die. It can kill.

Then the baby of sorrow inhales everything."

Hello air

Infinity is colonizing my mind

It's as if a cornerstone is familiar
but not the building

Is this illness, senility, amnesia, fatigue, wine,
medication or history

diminishing my memory

to the length of a bed?

Friends are often abandoned for passion
That Person walking the path I cut for him

from the elevator
to the hotel bar

His escape occurred
while no one was there to care.

The Gravity Bar was almost empty
except for him whom I didn't know

I lost my balance
because evil is aroused by absence

Outside on the island
a brick city had grown up and old

A person could only nibble on its shadows
Where was my one and only?

Somebody said:
"He's out of his bottle. . . . Mad as a bag of rats."

So then there was Arsene
beside the last remaining cabin
wandering with his eyes on the camera

Dynamite in his pocket
and a piece of thread
to trap a rabbit.

Love is a growing thing
It has its own sun
and never answers to the same name

Arsene held me in his arms
He was drunk as usual
and his nipple smelled of rum

But still I loved him as if he was the one.

If daily bread extends its quota
of air; and if heaven can't manage what earth can

If you are 55 degrees below zero and dying
there were no better times left!

When telephone wires are words trying
to be one sound—and the gray flannel sky

blurs on millions while they look forward
and no sense dares return empty

each container creates its fear of portion.

See the icy shape of a cowboy on a mirror?
Animals turned into legends—*The Tacky Little Lion*—

and silver bars
across the doors into the Church of Einstein?

Hail, curved time: "This labor camp is my cathedral."

The people head for work
at cow-crossing hour

There's a pale sun rising
On a backlash of milk and plastic

Step forward, step back

Anticipate mistrust
Remember regret

Disavow melancholy

Cemetery property's sanctified
by pedestrian ennui

Not remembered when there

Not with it either

A cloud cover uninscribed
like brother granite.

I know you won't believe me

But a man lifted his hand
and the top of his lip quivered
There was life in him
or something like it

It was as if brittle old
Lazarus snapped upright
Mary drew back
and baby was reaching

Or a copper bottle was
wiped free by a genie

It was a ton of stone
with the will to smile

I was east of my child
and six thousand miles
from my daughter's son
but I still loved them

Somewhere on the Sound
I imagine a ship's whistle sounds

and gray paint sparkles on a wet deck
The ocean is like biting an apple
Gray-textured foam

or a diamond in crumpled paper

I had to take the bus, there was no future.

Truth is very passive, even weak.
Who can survive without a plan?

Or an invention. Unfaithfulness can.

On my right hand the sun warms my pen.

The poets of my generation

and younger peck at the egg of the sky.
Blue shell, blue shell let all be well outside!

Tip-tip, won't crack . . . chip-chip, try try!

Where there is fertility, there is chaos.

A hundred years of turnover
and four generations later

we know everything about evil
in the public sphere

but what is a person
as a solitary seeker? How disassemble

the hypocritical
crippling factor in every body?

I couldn't tell the end
from the beginning
or one side from another
(west on the left?)

But I did seek structure
in a minute.

The models got smaller
the closer they were studied
too close I wiped my eyes
and cried.

This created
a problem for separating
the last impression from
the most ancient.

> Two shoes on a curtain
> Shadows thicker than a
> wax-white stripe.
> A floating paper bag
> colored rubber
> Drop-shaped leaves
> and silver lifted
> invisible thinking
> about terrible nothing:
> all in one blow.

If I look up
I see the end bends down
into today's eternity.

I am no one.
I know hell and have hope.

Let me travel the M11 down to Greystones
with my brother

as happy a soul as he is
and see the silver spears

of towers symbolically
built into the deep dream state.

Let me who? Who will let me?
Who am I addressing?

Time covered sky
over multiple eyes

A winter city's

ice is an oyster
inside a pearl.

A slow bus,
a frightened terrorist, a girl. . . .

My church is this machine rolling
the people along and sometimes

my church is a public latrine, sometimes
I drop on my knees and fall

across a chair like a coat in an empty room.

Sometimes I whisper *help*
to interrupt my wheeling brain.

I never learned how to live with a stranger
or an underground train.

Sometimes my church is a Franciscan chapel
near Penn Station. Beads rattle.

People sleep, mutter and curse.

When I leave this bus

a *thanks* to the driver is to cross and live

(for Maceo)

FANNY HOWE is a poet, fiction writer, essayist, and translator. She is the author of over twenty books, including *Selected Poems*, which won the 2001 Lenore Marshall Poetry Prize. She grew up in Boston and spent many years in California, New York City, and London. Currently she lives in New England. She has lived in the company of children for most of her life.

The text of *On the Ground* is set in a typeface known as Old Style Number Seven, which dates to a time when typefaces bore generic names rather than descriptive or fanciful ones. The roots of Old Style Number Seven can be found in the middle of the nineteenth century at the Miller & Richard type foundry in Edinburgh. At that time, Scottish founders led the way in cutting sturdy, even-colored types to meet the demands of new generations of printing presses. Down to the present day, Old Style Number Seven has continued to survive technology shifts.

This book was based on a design by Will Powers, set in type by Stanton Publication Services, Inc., and manufactured by Bang Printing on acid-free paper.